HOW TO PLAY BASS
PRACTICE IN YOUR DEAD TIME

ISBN NO: 978-1-7396648-8-6

HOW TO PLAY BASS DOT COM LTD

www.how-to-play-bass.com

Author Photo copyright Julie Kaye Photography

Thanks And Appreciations....

Writing books for me is a collaborative effort - thanks goes to the beta students who went on the journey with me:

John Fisher	Robert Weiman
Einar Sorensen	Charles Knight
Colin Baxter	Joshua Knisley
Andy Roberts	Wayne Pederson
Robert Cecchini	David Overton
Arthur Forgie	Richard Rosenbloom
Pete McCormick	Nigel Walden
Axel Knudsen	Alan Philpotts
Greg Chaseling	Curtis De La Cruz
Andrew Brandt	Ron Kramer
Robin Hoyles	John McIntyre
Manny Linares	Willie Munt
Joseph Krieg	Thomas Nelson
Andrew Crompton	Liz Patino
Scott Green	Steve Vinoski
Steve Kopercky	William Sederholm
Donna Eyman	George Wilcox
Michael Ashton	John Capello
Rob March	Steve Gilliland
Greg Jackson	Euan Coull
Keith Marfell	Steve Pullen
Ben Greer	Tiago Fauth
Steven Sellin	Stefan Schwarzenberger
Michael Siddall	John Gage
Brigid Blaschak	Andrew Williamson
Eric Pederson	Kim Jorgensen
Jason Bergschneider	Kit Koger
Malcolm Warner	Mark Slattery
David Gentry	James Koski
Meuryn Ioworth	Michael Bishop
Sean Baumann	Joseph Russo
Guy Berthelet	Paulia Allman
Bill Wenzel	Pierre Gervais
Eric Van De Wijer	John Smithers
Tim Peel	Carol Isen
Jon Jost	Robert Woodward
David Lescoe	John Wittig
Michael Bauer	Kevin Hulme
Joan Katis	

How To Use This Book

The printed copy of How To Play Bass - Practice In Your Dead Time has an online version that's free providedyou purchased your printed copy 'new' from Amazon and you send a copy of your Amazon receipt or invoice to my email address:

paul@how-to-play-bass.com

Full details and the four reasons why you should do this today can be found by turning to Page 95.

There are over 1000 pages of Random Rhythm Exercises to download and print out as and when you need them (see Section 6) as well as the expanding libraries of sight reading etudes (See Section 3 for their use as mental representation practice) and 'Wonky' sight reading etudes (see Section 4 for their use as mental representation practice.

There are other bonus items too that make the investment of the two minutes of your time to send the receipt or invoice copy to me worth your while.

Table Of Contents

Introduction

How To Play Bass - Practice In Your Dead Time is a companion volume to my book *Deliberate Practice 2.0 For Bass.* Note that having that volume is not a prerequisite to reading and using this volume.

There are some important ideas that inform both volumes though:

- All practice should be specifically aligned to, and dictated by, your bass goals.

- All practice should be logged in a practice diary.

- The main driver of improvement as a bass player is practicing material that is on the edge of your current ability level. (The 'Learning Zone.')

- Improvement only comes from purposeful or deliberate practice.

In the original study that led to Anders Ericsson codifying the principles of deliberate practice, violinists at the West Berlin School Of Music were split into three groups based on their ability levels. After detailed interviews with the students, their parents and teachers, and detailed investigation into their playing and practice habits, the study concluded there was one element that separated the top group of (excellent) students from the middle group of (very good) students from the bottom group of (good) students.

That element was the amount of practice hours logged. And specifically, the amount of deliberate practice hours logged by the students.

What leads from there is the corollary that the more deliberate practice you can do, the better you become as a bass player.

If you have time in your life to log two to three hours of deliberate practice on your bass every day, you're setting yourself up for constant and continuous improvement.

However, if you've got a job and a family and the kind of commitments that most of us have in 21st Century life, logging those two to three hours of deliberate practice every day can be challenging. (**Sidebar**: *typically two hours of deliberate practice takes up more than two hours of real time.*)

There are multiple ways of creating the time in your life to get in the practice and learning that you want to put in, and 'dead time' practice is one of those ways.

What Is 'Dead Time' Practice?

All of us have 'dead time' in our lives. For the purposes of this book there are two principle chunks of 'dead time' to look for that could be used for bass practice activities (even if you don't have your bass with you):

- Activities where the body is busy, but the brain is not. Examples of this are driving, traveling on public transport (bus, train, plane), the gym, running, 'chore' type activities like gardening or digging.

- Time where you're sat somewhere with either nothing to do or nothing specific to do. E.g. your lunch hour at work. Waiting at the dentist or doctors! Waiting in the car to pick up a child from school.

All of these periods in our lives can be made more productive by using them for the kind of 'dead time' practice activities that this volume will address.

Can You Improve On Bass Without Your Bass?

The short answer is yes. The long answer is also yes.

There are certain practice activities that you can do that don't require your bass. Some quick examples:

- Analyzing bass lines to improve your understanding of how bass lines are put together (Sections 3 and 4).

- Working on your understand of rhythmic sub-divisions (Section 6).

- Working on your internal clock by tapping or clapping (Sections 1 and 2).

- Visualization (Section 9).

And so on.

This volume will give you specific examples of the kind of exercises you can do to make productive use of your dead time, as well as dead time practice principles so you can create your own exercises that align with your practice goals.

That leads to an important caveat that is repeated multiple times throughout this volume as it's so mission critical:

- All practice you do - whether 'dead time' practice or regular practice - should be aligned with your practice goals. Those goals should inform a practice plan that aims to take you from where you are now as a bass player to where you want to get to as a bass player.

Note though:

If You Can Practice With A Bass...That Tends To More Beneficial

As a generalization, practice with your bass in hand is more beneficial than practice without it. Though some of the activities in this volume can be started without your bass and you can then graduate to your bass (e.g. Internal Clock exercises, rhythmic precision exercises).

The whole purpose of this volume is to give you ideas for how you can use the periods that all of us have in our lives where we're not productive. And just as your dead time practice should align with your goals, it should also support your bass playing practice and be an extension of it.

Also note some of the activities suggested can be done at home, even in your practice space, at times that are not 'dead time' periods as suggested on the page previously. Specifically, I'm thinking of supporting activities like periodic practice reviews and practice plan maintenance and the like.

The Practice Activities Suggested In This Volume Are There For A Reason

If you download and read the first iteration of this book, binge written in 2013 if memory serves, you'll see that the first iteration features a range of suggested activities that are effectively a randomly chosen collection.

In the 10 years between the writing of the two books I've come up with the concept of the 80-20 Bass Vocabulary and have been codifying it device by device over that period. And came to the realization that for 99% of bass players this is the most important information they should be studying, learning and assimilating.

Learning the bass through the lens of 80-20 Bass leads you to focus on bass lines for songs.The majority of this volume uses the musical elements needed to play bass lines to songs as an organizing framework.

The first two sections cover working on your internal clock. Having a strong internal clock is something few teachers talk about, yet is one of the most foundational skills to have in your toolbox. And it is something you can work on and improve. Having a great 'groove' when playing lines - even if only simple quarter notes - comes down to this.

Similarly the mental representations sections will help you work on improving your understanding of bass lines to songs, what goes into them, how you can take small ideas from a bass line to your practice space to add them to your vocabulary, and more.

And so on. Every section is directly connected to understanding and/or developing the skills needed to play bass lines to songs.

If you were to ask which sections are the most important, my answer would be:

- Sections 1 and 2. Internal Clock.

- Sections 3 and 4. Mental Representations Of Bass Lines.

• Section 6. Precision with rhythmic sub-divisions.

For the majority of students reading this book, I guarantee that if you invest 10 hours of dead time practice with each of those sections you *will* improve as a bass player.

Note one of the byproducts of identifying those kind of activities to work on as dead time practice: it forces you to isolate the core of the activity and focus on just that. Sometimes, especially when developing facility, the bass is another layer that gets in the way of assimilation.

Dead Time Practice Should Be Logged Just Like Bass Practice

When you start doing dead time practice, make sure you log it in your practice plan and that it gets incorporated into your weekly planning sheets, your daily practice logs, and your periodic reviews.

The process of planning for dead time practice, doing it, and logging it also teaches your brain this is important and that you're not just goofing around.

How To Use This Book

Although there are some theoretical ideas in this book, it's intended to be a guide for you to implement dead time practice into your life so that you can take invest time where you can't be practicing with your bass in hand into making you a better bass player and a better musician.

Every student reading this will have a unique combination of their current ability level and their current bass goals. So it's impossible to write a book that caters to typical groups of bassists, as by definition those typical groups don't exist.

Here's how I recommend you use this book:

1. Identify What Dead Time You Have In Your Life, How Much of It, And Where That Is.

The primary areas in people's lives where they have dead time are: commuting to and from work; lunch time or similar down time at a place of work; regular activity that involves the body but not the brain (e.g. the gym, swimming, household stuff, walking the dog, and so on).

2. Identify What Kind Of Dead Time Practice You Can Do.

Each of the above scenarios lend themselves to different kind of activities, so you need to identify what kind of scenario you have as that dictates what kind of dead time practice you can do.

3. Align Your Dead Time Practice With Your Bass Playing Goals.

The exercises I suggest throughout this volume are suggestions and examples of the kind of the thing you can do, not prescriptive exercises that you must do. Like all practice, don't practice or learn something because a teacher has suggested an exercise that is 'cool.' Instead, run any practice suggestions through this question as a filter:

"Does this activity lead me towards my bass goals?"

If the answer is no, then that practice idea should be junked. (Although note that if your goals change, that practice idea might need to be reassessed.)

I've tried to cover possible practice activities in this volume that will benefit most bassists. E.g. working on your internal clock, working on your mental representations of bass lines, creating your own practice exercises, working on your perception of rhythmic sub-divisions and so on.

As mentioned, you combination of your current ability level and current goals is unique. So choose exercises that align with getting you from where you are to where you want to get to be. If some of the suggested exercises in this volume need to be adapted, then adapt them. If you need to create your own exercises, then use my suggested exercises as guidelines and create your own exercises that will help you achieve your unique goals. If you're unsure, you can always drop me an email.

4. Create/Gather The Material you Need For Dead Time Practice.

Your dead time practice will require some supporting practice material. Whether that's print outs of rhythms. Or MP3 practice tracks. Or ear training tracks. Create anything that needs creating. Collate anything that you have that you need.

5. Start Including Dead Time Practice In Your Practice Schedule - And Start Logging It.

Dead time practice is practice. So treat it as such. Start planning for it. Start noting it down on your practice sheets. Start including it in your review sessions.

Remember two things: (i) if you only add 30 minutes of dead time practice to your schedule, five days a week, that's around an extra 125 hours of practice logged over the next year; (ii) the principle element that separates musicians in qualitative terms is hours of deliberate practice logged.

In 10 years time you'll have logged an additional 1250 hours. That's probably more than the amount of practice most 'ordinary' students log. If you want to be ordinary, then forget dead time practice. If you want to achieve your bass playing goals, dead time practice accelerates that process.

Section 1 - Internal Clock Exercises (Part 1)

Exercises that practice on improving your 'internal clock' improve your sense of time. These exercises can be done with your bass in hand, and full details of different ways to do this can be found in *Time And Groove For Bass Guitar*, but there are exercises you can do to work on this when you're away from your bass.

As noted in the introduction, one of this book's goals is to give as many dead time exercises as possible that you can do straight away, as well as outlining dead time practice principles.

If you've got a device capable of loading MP3 files to, a pair of headphones, and access to the online version of the book (see page 3 for how to get that), then you can jump to the online version of Section 1, download the files and get started today with the first set of exercises.

Exercise 1 - Internal Clock Audit Exercise

Internal clock exercises use metronomic tracks with a difference. That difference is that, unlike conventional metronome exercises, not every beat is represented by a metronome click.

This forces you to be responsible for the beats not covered by the metronome. And the beats that are covered by a metronome click serve as audit points so that you can check that you are still in time.

This first exercise is to help you audit how good your current perception of time is, and identify precisely what you need to work on. Here's a music graphic that represents what's happening and then I'll explain how you use this exercise:

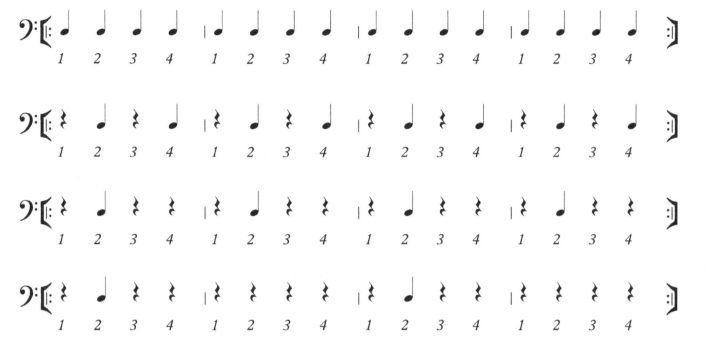

This is a 32 bar exercise and, after the two bar count in used on every practice track, it's comprised of:

- 8 bars where the metronome click sounds on every beat.

- 8 bars where the metronome click sounds on beat 2 and 4 only.

- 8 bars where the metronome click sounds on beat 2 only.

- 8 bars where the metronome click sounds on beat 2 every other bar.

This exercise initially shouldn't be a dead time exercise, you use it to identify how good your sense of internal time is.

If you can set the slow version of this track playing and count along with every beat and be precisely in time with the drum that sounds on the downbeat of bar 33, then you can either move to the next section of the book, or check out the two advanced exercises. I've provided tracks at different tempo levels though, start out with the 120 BPM track and see how you fare. Then try the 100 BPM track. And then the 80 BPM track.

In bars 9 to 16, where the metronome clicks on beats 2 and 4, you're responsible for keeping the time for every other beat, so beats 1 and 3. If this section gives you a problem, then jump to exercises 2 and 3.

In bars 17 to 24, where the metronome clicks on beat 2 only, you're responsible for keeping the time for beats 1, 3 and 4 in every bar. If this section gives you a problem, then jump to exercise 4 and 5.

In bars 25 to 32, where the metronome clicks on beat 2 every other bar, you're responsible for keeping the time for 7 beats out of every bar. If this is the section that gives you a problem, jump to exercises 6 and 7.

Exercises 2 and 3

These 32 bar exercises are designed to start working on the area you identified as a weakness when using exercise 1 as an audit exercise.

Exercise 2 looks like this:

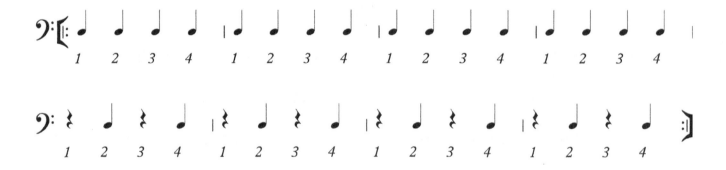

This exercise has four bars where the metronome click sounds on every beat, and then four bars where it sounds on beats 2 and 4 only. This 8 bar sequence repeats four times.

There are tracks for exercise 2 at 120 BPM, 100 BPM and 80 BPM. Your goal is to set this playing, and tap your hand to the beat. The audit points to be aware of here are:

- Making sure your hand tap is in time with the clicks on beats 2 and 4 on the second four bars of every 8 bar repeat.

- Making sure your hand tap is in time with the downbeat every time you transition to the section where the metronome click sounds on every beat.

When you are comfortable with exercise 2, then try out exercise 3:

Play 8 Times

Every bar in exercise 3, apart from the two bar count-in, has the metronome click on beats 2 and 4. As before, these tracks are provided at 120 BPM, 100 BPM and 80 BPM. Start with the 120 BPM track and progress to the 100 BPM track and finally the 80 BPM track.

Sidebar *although exercise 1 is primarily designed to identify which internal clock exercises you should work on, as you start working on these exercises you can go back to it from time to time to verify that your internal clock is improving! If you do that, make sure you make a note of this however you track your practice.*

When you are comfortable with the 80 BPM track, it's time for exercises 4 and 5.

Exercises 4 and 5

These 32 bar exercises are designed to start working on the area you identified as a weakness when using exercise 1 as an audit exercise, or following on from working with exercises 2 and 3.

Exercise 4 looks like this:

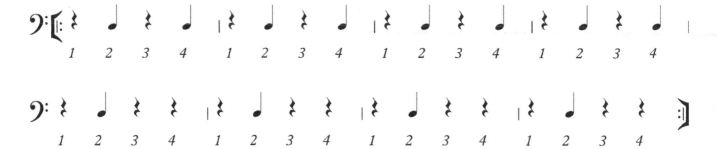

This exercise has four bars where the metronome click sounds on beats 2 and 4 only, and then four bars where it sounds on beat 2 only. This 8 bar sequence repeats four times.

There are tracks for exercise 4 at 120 BPM, 100 BPM and 80 BPM. Your goal is to set this playing, and tap your hand to the beat. The audit points to be aware of here are:

- Making sure your hand tap is in time with the clicks on beats 2 and 4 on the first four bars of every 8 bar repeat.

- Making sure your hand tap is in time with the clicks on beat 2 of the second four bars of every 8 bar repeat.

When you are comfortable with exercise 4, then try out exercise 5:

Play 8 times

If you find exercise 5 hard, then use exercise 4 to build proficiency by having the four bars where the metronome clicks on beats 2 and 4 to fall back on.

When you're comfortable with the 80 BPM tracks for exercise 5, then you can move onto exercises 6 and 7.

Exercises 6 and 7

These 32 bar exercises are designed to start working on the area you identified as a weakness when using exercise 1 as an audit exercise, or following on from working on the previous exercises.

Exercise 6 looks like this:

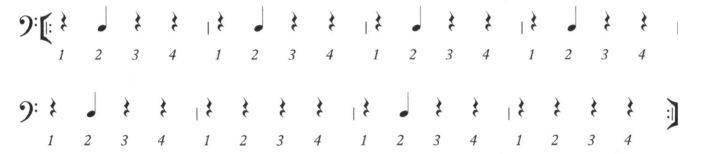

This exercise has four bars where the metronome click sounds on beat 2 only, and then four bars where it sounds on beat 2 every other bar. This 8 bar sequence repeats four times.

There are tracks for exercise 6 at 120 BPM, 100 BPM and 80 BPM. Your goal is to set this playing, and tap your hand to the beat. The audit points to be aware of here are:

  • Making sure your hand tap is in time with the clicks on beats 2 in the first four bars of every 8 bar repeat.

  • Making sure your hand tap is in time with the clicks on beat 2 of every other bar in the second four bars of every 8 bar repeat.

When you are comfortable with exercise 6, then try out exercise 7:

Advanced Exercises - 8 and 9

If you can successfully count through exercise 7, that means you have a strong sense of time and can reliably track8 beats worth of time. That's good. If you want to work on the next level then try out exercise 9 that combines playing for 4 bars with a click on beat 2 every other bar with 4 bars where you get the click on beat two just once!

Here's what that exercise looks like:

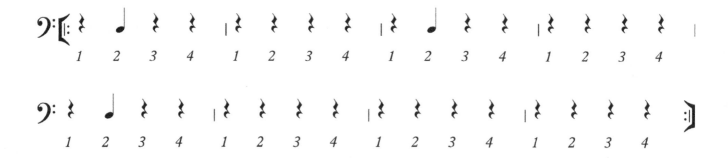

The progression from there is exercise 9 where you get a count in and then a click on beat 2 of the first bar of every four bars:

If you can successfully maintain time for 16 beats of rest, then your internal clock is in great shape. Many professional musicians can't do this. As mentioned in the introduction, further practice of this kind may cease to be as effective in meeting your bass playing goals as other exercises.

Summary

Having a strong sense of time is an important part of the bass player's toolkit. The exercises contained in this section will help you develop that strong 'internal clock.' More importantly, they can be done whenever you've got 15 minutes or so of spare time but you don't have your bass to hand.

Use the first track to identify how many beats you can successfully track when the metronome clicks start to drop out. And be ruthlessly honest about where you are comfortable and where you are finding it difficult. Then you can target that difficulty. The first exercise in each pair is designed to combine 4 bars where you are comfortable, and then 4 bars that are challenging.

Don't expect to progress to exercise 9 overnight. But if you practice regularly, you'll be amazed at how much progress you can achieve in three months. As your sense of internal time improves, that will have a subtle, but profound, impact on your bass playing.

Section 2 - Internal Clock Exercises (Part 2)

Directly following on from Section 1, in Section 2 is another series of exercises that you can use to work on your internal clock. They are similar to the exercises in Section 1. In Section 1 the exercises worked on the '2 and 4' series of beats, but in Section 2 the exercises work on the 'drop' series of beats.

There's an internal clock audit exercise to get started with that will introduce this concept and allow you to pinpoint where your internal clock is currently set so that you can select exercises that are in your learning zone (i.e. they help you improve) and not in your comfort zone (i.e. you can already do these exercises.)

Exercise 10 - Internal Clock Audit Exercise 2

The internal clock exercise for Section 2 uses the drop series, there's a representation of the exercise on the next page but the exercise works like this:

- The drop series audit exercise is 64 bars long, divided into 8 bar sections.

- In the first 8 bars, the last beat of bars 4 and 8 is 'dropped.' Your job is to count through and ensure that you hit the downbeat on bars 5 and 9 with no problems.

- In the second 8 bar section, beats 3 and 4 of bars 4 and 8 of that section are dropped. Again your job is to ensure you hit the following downbeats in time.

- Every 8 bars, another beat is dropped so that the amount of beats that you are responsible increases. Your job is always to hit the following downbeat.

- The last 8 bars has 8 beats that you are responsible for.

Here's a representation of the exercise that you can count along with:

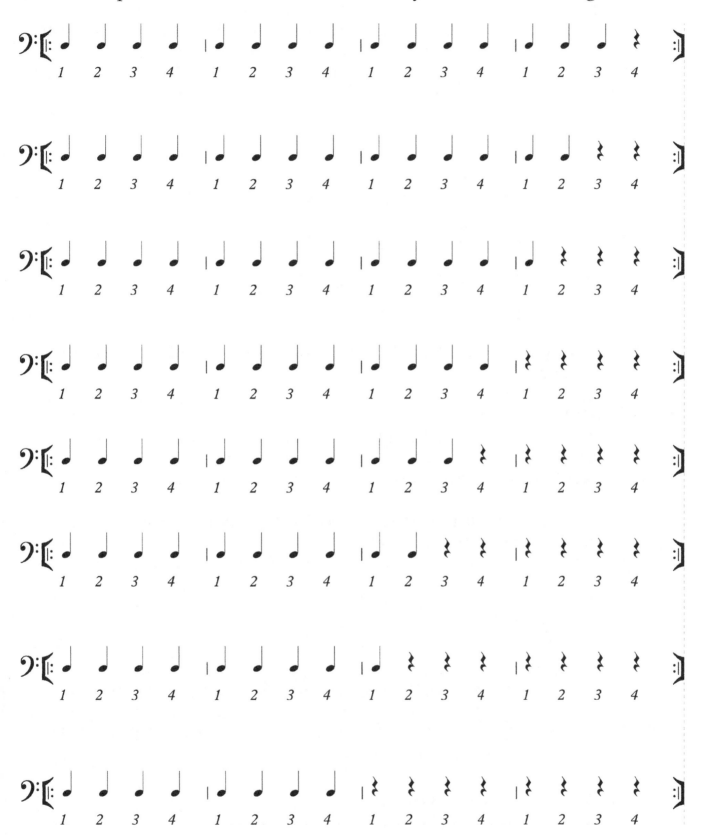

Counting through this exercise will identify how many beats your 'internal clock' is set to confidently count through. Either you hit the downbeat confidently in each 8 bar section or you don't. When you find a section where you don't, then see how many beats you were responsible for. If it was five, then 'warm up' with the Drop 4 exercise below and then cue up the Drop 5 exercise and work with that until you're comfortable.

Your goals for this Section are:

- Identify how many beats you can confidently track. And where your internal clock starts to struggle. The audit point to use is if you don't hit the downbeat after the beats of silence. Use the MP3 track for Exercise 10 for this.

- Identify and name what you need to work on. If you struggle with dropping 5 beats, that's the Drop 5 exercise.

- Warm up with the Drop 4 exercise and then switch to the Drop 5 exercise.

- Starting out, you may need to switch between Drop 4 - where you are comfortable - and then Drop 5. With dead time practice, your internal clock will improve. The number of times you need to switch to Drop 4 will lessen.

- When you're feeling confident of Drop 5, take the audit exercise again and see if you are ready to continue the process with Drop 6.

Exercise 11 - Drop 2

Each of the following exercises are 32 bar exercises, In the Drop 2 exercise, beats 3 and 4 of every fourth bar are dropped. The downloadable MP3 tracks for each exercise are provided at 120 BPM, 100 BPM and 80 BPM. Start with the 120 BPM tempo, and progress to 80 BPM. (With these exercises, the slower they are the harder they are.)

Here's what the Drop 2 exercise looks like:

Exercise 12 - Drop 3

In the Drop 3 exercise beats 2, 3 and 4 of every fourth bar are dropped. Here's what the Drop 3 Exercise looks like:

Exercise 13 - Drop 4

In the Drop 4 exercise beats 1, 2, 3 and 4 of every fourth bar are dropped. Here's what the Drop 4 Exercise looks like:

Exercise 14 - Drop 5

In the Drop 5 exercise beat 4 of every third bar, and all the beats of every fourth bar, are dropped. Here's what the Drop 5 Exercise looks like:

Exercise 15 - Drop 6

In the Drop 6 exercise beats 3 and 4 of every third bar, and all the beats of every fourth bar, are dropped. Here's what the Drop 6 Exercise looks like:

Exercise 16 - Drop 7

In the Drop 7 exercise beats 2, 3 and 4 of every third bar, and all the beats of every fourth bar , are dropped. Here's what the Drop 7 Exercise looks like:

Exercise 17 - Drop 8

In the Drop 8 all the beats of every third and fourth bar are dropped. Here's what the Drop 8 Exercise looks like:

Advanced Exercises

You can go beyond this and create a series of tracks to take you all the way to Drop 16. The starting point to target though is being able to count through 8 beats of silence. As mentioned in Section 1, if you can do that your internal sense of time has to be strong. That internal sense of time will show up in your playing too which it's why it's worth doing these exercises.

Summary

The exercises contained in this section are similar to the exercises in Section 1 and are designed to help you develop a strong 'internal clock.'

The exercises in Section 2 approach working on your internal clock from a different perspective. The sequential way that beats are 'dropped' suits some people more than the '2 and 4' series. Going beyond 8 beats of silence can be done sequentially much easier with the 'drop series' than with the '2 and 4' series.

As with Section 1, use the first track in this series to identify how many beats you can successfully track when the metronome clicks drop out. And use that identification to select drop series exercises designed to work on exactly that spot.

The exercises in Sections 1 and 2 may seem basic - in some ways they are - but the effect they have on your playing is worth the investment of practice time. Especially as this is 'dead time' when you don't have your bass to hand. These two sections were deliberately placed at the front of this volume as I believe these are the dead time exercises that will have the most impact on your bass playing

Section 3 - Mental Representations Of Bass Lines (Part 1)

Mental Representations are dealt with in detail in ***Deliberate Practice for Bass Guitar 2.0***. The one sentence summary is this: *mental representations are like a mental map that your brain creates when exposed to repeated study or repeated practice.*

Chess is a field of study for researchers investigating mental representations. One striking fact they found was the difference between an average player and a grand master wasn't higher IQ or a better memory, it was the number and detail of the mental representations of the game that they had.

For every move, an average chess player might have ten permutations that he could try out at specific points in the game. Contrast that with a Grandmaster who would have hundreds of permutations to use at that point of the game. Or thousands.

Those mental representations were built up by studying chess games. In exactly the same way, you can build better (and more detailed) mental representations of bass lines by studying bass lines.

That study can be done without your bass to hand. So it makes a perfect dead time practice activity.

Studying bass lines is one of the most high leverage practice activities that exists for bass players. Here's the elements you can target, which leads to more detailed mental representations of bass lines:

- What devices great players use, and on what chords.

- What rhythms they use to execute those devices.

- What devices they use to connect specific chord movements.

- What modifying devices they use.

- How they use advanced ideas like modifying devices, indirect resolutions, slash chords, pedal tones, double stops and so on.

- Ideas that you find, and that you decide you like the sound of, can then be isolated and turned into practice exercises to help you assimilate those ideas. That creation of practice exercises can also be done without your bass to hand. (See Section 5.)

This dead time practice activity only requires that you have accurate transcriptions of bass lines, a pencil, and 10 to 15 minutes to sit quietly somewhere to study that bass line, or sections of it. This kind of study helps build more detailed mental representations of how bass lines are put together.

Here's an example that I'm going to walk through so you can see the kind of process you can use. Here's a twelve bar blues rock progression with a Tommy Shannon style bass line:

When presented with a line like this, most students simply play through it and work it up to tempo. And that's it. Which is a waste because the majority of the information that's contained in just this twelve bar section is overlooked.

So two things to immediately note:

- You don't have to start out with a complete bass line. You can get started with sub-sections of a line.

- To fully understand what's happening in this line you need to analyze it and work out how each of the notes are functioning in terms of their relationship against the harmony, which leads to the commonly used ideas in bass lines that I've been codifying through the years as 80-20 Bass.

Here's this twelve bar fragment analyzed:

Once you've analyzed a section of a bass line, here are all the different areas you could look into to build your mental representations of how bass lines are put together:

- What devices has the bass player used?

- What rhythmic level are the devices being used at? Does a device play out over a complete bar? Or is the player using the concept of front end and back end (beats 1 and 2 is the front end, beats 3 and 4 is the back end)? More rarely, is a complete device used on a single beat?

- What are the chords used in the progression - what two chord movements are contained within the overall progression.

- What devices are used to move from one chord to the next?

- What rhythms are being used to execute the devices being played? (Note this is a different question than what rhythmic level the devices are being played at.)

- Are any modifying devices used? If so, how?

- Are any connecting devices being used to strengthen how the line connects from one chord to the next?

One of my mantras is: all practice (even dead time practice) should be aligned with your bass playing goals. So your goals may modify that list of questions and focus this kind of practice.

Sidebar: *though my advice throughout this book is that any practice you do aligns with your practice goals, a case can be made for building detailed mental representations of how bass lines are put together by analyzing complete sections of great bass lines in detail IF this is an area that you've not yet studied.*

Depending on how you analyze lines, here's a list of the elements that have gone into this bass line that you could pull out:

Devices (bar by bar):

- R-3-5-Ch.

- 8-3-4-Ch.

- R-3-5-3.

- R-3-5-Ch.

- 8-b7-6-5

- R-3-4-Ch.

- 8-6-5-3.

- R-3-4-Ch.

- R-3-R-Ch.

- 8-b7-6-Ch.

- 8-3-4-Ch.

- R-2-b3-3.

Rhythmic Level: All devices are played at a quarter note level - the four device notes of each device note can be seen on every quarter note beat.

Two Chord Movements Used:

C7 to F7; F7 to C7; C7 to C7; F7 to F7; C7 to G7; G7 to F7; G7 to C7. Note that the chord movements of C7 to C7, and F7 to F7, have the same intervallic root movement. So do the two chord progressions of G7 to C7 and C7 to F7. And also the F7 to C7, and C7 to G7 two chord progression.

Chord Movements/Devices:

- C7 to F7 (and G7 to C7): R-3-5-Ch; R-2-b3-3.

- F7 to C7 (and C7 to G7): 8-3-4-Ch; R-3-4-Ch; 8-b7-6-Ch.

- C7 to C7 (and F7 to F7): R-3-5-3; 8-b7-6-5; 8-6-5-3.

- G7 to F7: R-3-R-Ch.

Rhythms Used To Execute The Devices

Although the devices are played at a quarter note level, the rhythms used to execute them are pairs of swing 8th note for each of those quarter note device notes. And there's one triplet on the downbeat of bar 11.

Modifying Devices:

The modifying devices used include the root bounce (bar 8); muted notes (bars 9 and 10); an 8-5-8 triplet (downbeat of bar 11), and the variation to the R-3-4-ch device on the back end of bar 11 could be considered as a modifying device.

Connecting Devices:

The chromatic approach notes at the end of bars 1 and 4 could be considered as connecting device modifiers to standard R-3-5 major triad ideas.

That's only one 12 bar segment of a bass line. Analyzing it like this helps understand what goes into putting a solid bass line together.

We live in an age of plenty and there are now thousands of good quality, commercially available transcriptions of bass lines featuring players like James Jamerson, Paul McCartney, Duck Dunn, Flea, John Paul Jones, Geddy Lee, Marcus Miller, Rocco Prestia, Jaco Pastorius and so on.

Building a transcription library is something every bass player who aspires to improve should do. Analyzing sections of lines in the manner outlined above helps unlock the 'secrets' hidden in those lines.

Billy Sheehan said: *"The answers to your bass playing questions can be found in the grooves of your record collection."* When Billy was learning there were no transcription books, no Internet swamped with (inaccurate) tabs and no Internet sites where you can purchase accurate transcriptions and download them 10 seconds later.

The contemporary version of that quote could be reworded to: *"The answers to your bass playing questions can be found in the bars of your transcription library."*

That transcription library is only a valuable resource if you use it. The first step is to isolate sections and analyze them.

Sidebar 1: 5 Transcription Books For Your Library

As with all bass endeavors, your transcription library should align with your practice goals. So if you're an aspiring country and folk bass player you probably don't need to study the lines of Jaco Pastorius.

The counter argument is that the principles of good bass playing and good bass line construction apply across genres. So if you analyze a Jaco line and find unique ways of connecting two chords together (for example), there's no reason why that couldn't be used in a country bass setting with appropriate changes in rhythmic execution of the idea to make it genre appropriate.

My advice is: start with building detailed mental representations of bass lines by studying the acknowledged masters, and then narrow the focus by studying the masters of your chosen genre(s).

The 5 transcription books I recommend for your library for the purpose of analyzing in order to build your mental representations of how bass lines are put together are:

- *Standing In The Shadows Of Motown*. This is a collection of James Jamerson transcriptions. The great thing about studying Jamerson is that his playing developed over a number of years at Motown. So if you organize the transcriptions into chronological order then you can track Jamerson's development as a player.

- *Paul McCartney Transcriptions*. The Beatles Complete Scores has transcriptions of everything the Beatles put out. Or you could start with the 'Off The Record' transcriptions of the two greatest hits albums. Like Jamerson, McCartney's playing changed and developed over a number of years and those two books give a reasonable overview of that, though there are recommended performances missing (like '*Rain*' and '*The Word*').

- *Rush The Complete Scores.* There are 40 complete songs scored out in this volume. As with the previous two suggestions, analyzing lines in this book allows you to get a chronological overview of how Geddy's bass playing has changed and developed over time.

- *Bass Bible Series.* This is a series of six books that groups transcriptions by genre. So you've got Funk, Rock, Pop-Rock, Hard Rock, R&B and Slap versions. Each book has around thirty transcriptions, so you could use these genre themed books to look for recurring devices and rhythms within genres.

- *Transcriptions Of Your Favourite Player.* I've probably not mentioned your favourite player. There may be books of your idol (or idols) available. If not, either transcribe some of their lines yourself or - depending on your skills - you could commission someone else to transcribe these lines. Then study them!

Precision Analysis

The kind of analysis framework used for the blues rock style example on pages 28 and 29 can be used in any genre to help build your overall mental representations of how good bass lines are put together.

You can also use dead time to do 'precision analysis' of sections of bass lines. Billy Sheehan's quote from the previous page - *"The answers to your bass playing questions can be found in the bars of your transcription library"* - can apply on a micro level as well as a macro level.

The 'macro' level is to look at complete song performances, or complete sections as already demonstrated. The 'micro' level is to go through your transcriptions and look for specific answers to specific questions.

Imagine you were playing at a blues jam at the weekend and wanted to add some ideas to elevate your playing at that jam. You could take a few transcriptions of blues rock bass lines and look through for specific ideas that can be added to your vocabulary. Areas you could look at include (but are not limited to):

- *Bar 9 ideas*. Can you find new ways of connecting the V7 and IV7 chords?

- *Triplet modifying devices*. An easy way to add rhythmic and harmonic variety to your vocabulary is to add three or four triplet modifying devices.

- *Stop verse ideas*. Most blues rock tunes contain stop verses - comb through your transcriptions to find not only the melodic patterns used within the stop sections, but how the stop sections are set up and how the bass line transitions back to normal playing.

- *Setting up bars that start with the 5th or the 3rd*. Not every bar has to start with the root note, in blues rock (especially solo sections). Look through your transcriptions to see how that is done and cross reference to what kind of song section it's done on (e.g. on a vocal section, or only on solo sections).

You can use precision analysis to get more specific than this. The kind of things you can could look for with precision analysis to give you further examples are:

- Ways of connecting specific chord movements. E.g. C to Eb (or an ascending minor third...doesn't matter what the key is.)

- Back end devices that don't start on the root - and you could go further and categorize these by the interval between the root of the chord (played on the front end of the bar) and the root of the next chord.

- Unusual modifying devices.

- Devices played at a 16th note level.

- Devices layered onto each other.

- Use of double stops.

- Bass line ideas for slash chords.

And so on.

When you identify an idea that solves a musical problem you have, then you can turn that into a practice exercise (also in your dead time - see Section 5) so that it can be added to your daily and/or weekly practice plan (see Section 7).

Not only does precision analysis improve your mental representations of bass line, but it gives you fuel for your practice which then leads to incremental ability gains. And the practice that you do will cement the learning further and strengthen your mental representations. All of which forms a virtuous cycle.

Sidebar 2: Precision Analysis And Transcription

For students who want to improve in the long term (so thinking forwards at least 3 years) one of the best things they can do to support that goal is build up a transcription library. I've given suggestions earlier in this section of published transcription as well as mentioning commissioning transcriptions as a further source to get specific material into your library.

Obviously you can also transcribe bass lines yourself, but depending on your goals, and how good you are at transcribing, it may make more sense to pay someone else to transcribe for you so that your time is freed up for direct practice.

One of the ways you can keep the cost down is to commission someone just to transcribe sections from songs where you're using precision analysis. With the previous example of looking for ways bass players have connected two chords whose roots are an ascending minor third apart (e.g. C to Eb), what you could do is commission transcription of either short sections of songs (like verses), or even just two bar sections of songs that contain this chord progresion.

For precision analysis of this chord movement that could mean asking for transcriptions of all the choruses for '50 Ways To Leave Your Lover,' all the verses of 'Suicide Blonde,' all the verses of 'Long Cool Woman In A Black Dress,' the verses of 'Purple Haze' and 'I Am A Walrus' and 'Higher Ground' and so on.

By doing this, you preserve your practice time - although transcribing is a high value practice activity for intermediate and above level students - and you'll get multiple bars that you can use precision analysis with to provide answers to the musical question(s) you have.

Section 4 - Mental Representations Of Bass Lines (Part 2)

In Section 3 the concept of analyzing bass lines to build up your mental representation of how good bass lines are put together was introduced. The primary way you do this is by taking published transcriptions and identifying the devices that went into that bassline and all the associated information (rhythms, how devices are used to connect chords, modifying devices, etc.).

There's a secondary way you can do this, that's arguably quicker. (There's a caveat though.)

That secondary way involves taking bass lines that don't work, analyzing them to find out why they don't work, and correcting them. The caveat of course is that 'bass lines that don't work' don't get recorded and don't get transcribed and published in transcription books.

I'll outline two ways to solve that problem that in a moment. Let's work through an example first.

Let's say you found this 8 bar section in a published bass line:

Depending on how finely tuned your mental representations of devices and bass lines are, you might know that there are major problems with this line just by looking at the notation.

If not, that's something you can use your dead time practice to work on.

The first step is to analyze what devices are used in this 8 bar line, and also check to see if there are solid connections at the end of each bar. Here's that analysis added to the 8 bar line:

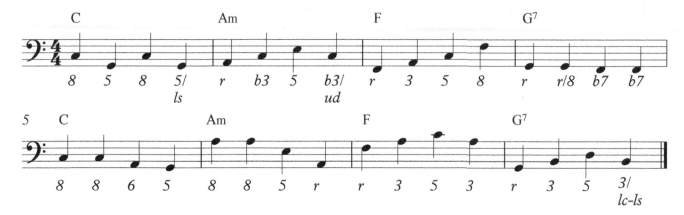

All of the devices used work for the specific bar they are in. There are no glaring issues like minor thirds being played on major chords (or vice versa). Of the eight bars in this example, there are only three bars where the device connects to the root note of the next bar in a logical manner.

Let's work through how you could fix this line. Whenever I do this my goal is to fix a line with as few changes as possible and not take the 'easy' fix of replacing a device that doesn't lead to the root (or target) note on the next downbeat.

Here's how I'd set this up in my music pad:

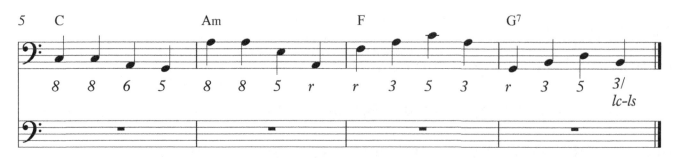

Looking at the analyzed example, the first two bars work well and lead to the root note of the next bars. So I'd copy those first two bars along with the root note of the third bar:

Bar 3 uses a R-3-5-8 device and that doesn't connect to the root note of the G7 chord in bar 4. There are two options: you can change the last note of the device in bar 3 so that the root note of bar 4 sounds logical (e.g. R-3-5-R), or; you can change the placement of the root note of bar 4 so that it sounds logical. I've gone for the latter choice:

Neither choice is 'right' or better than the other. Ultimately as you do this kind of exercise more and create your own bass lines you'll find that there are certain ideas you like the sound of and gravitate towards.

That's a normal part of a bass player's evolution and you should embrace that. Knowing what you like and using those ideas more in your playing starts to create a unique way to approach creating bass lines that will eventually become recognizably 'your sound.'

The reason I chose to lift the G an octave was that I was looking ahead at the device used in bar 4 and how I would connect that to the C root note on the downbeat of bar 5.

And to do that I decided to transpose all 4 notes in bar 4 and then change the b7 on beat 4 to a fifth to connect to the root note of C. Like this:

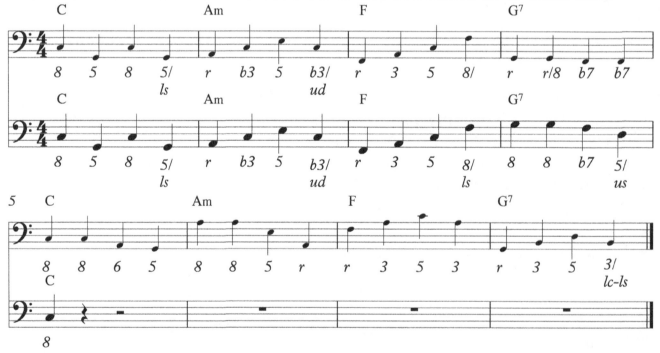

In bar 5 the 8-8-6-5 device will connect to the root note of Am, but an octave lower than where it's currently played:

Looking forwards to the remaining three bars, I don't want to change bar 8 at all because that was one of the three original bars that worked well. So that likely means the major triad on the F chord (bar 7) will need to be transposed down an octave. Let's put those onto the notation:

A quick side note: that last note of bar 7 works. But there's a case to be made for making the device in bar 7 the R-3-5-R device which has more harmonic movement in the device but still connects the F and G7 bars together with a scalar approach note. This is a stylistic choice and the simple way to find out what you prefer the sound of is to play both variations and see which sounds best to your ears.

Onto bar 6. The purpose of this exercise is to 'fix' the line and change as few notes as possible. The simplest way to do that is to drop beats 2 and 3 of bar 6 an octave and change beat 4 to another '5.' Like this:

If the original line is now stripped away, the edited line that's left looks like this:

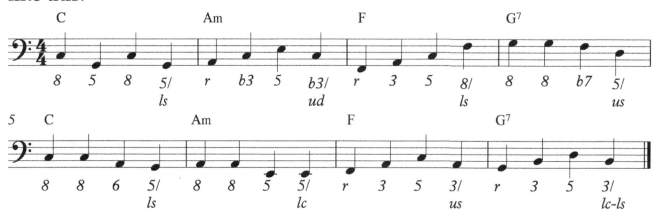

The benefit of doing this kind of exercise is that it will improve both the number and the quality of your mental representations of what goes into creating/playing a good bass line. Which in turn feeds into your playing when creating your own lines or playing other player's lines (and improving them).

One problem though: that there are no 'transcription books' of poor bass lines available that you can use to correct. As promised at the start of this section there are two ways to produce 'poor bass lines' so that you can fix them.

Method 1 is to use Band In A Box. As you probably know, I'm a big fan of this program. Though it's not created specifically for bass players there are plenty of ways that the program can be tweaked to help our practice.

I've created Band In A Box styles to help bass players generate good quality sight reading etudes and bass lines. To produce poor bass lines I made a copy of some of those styles and then tweaked the formating so that Band In A Box chooses devices in a way that creates poor lines. That can then be edited using music notation software to present a 'double score' like the example of Page 37.

If you don't possess Band In A Box, then you can create 'poor bass lines' manually using notation paper and a deck of cards to work as a randomizer.

Here's how that would work - and you can tailor this to your specific needs:

- Take a random 8 or 16 bar chord progression from a songbook.

- Write the chords out on music paper.

- Take a deck of cards and assign 10 devices to the 10 number cards. E.g. the Ace represents roots and fifths in quarter notes, the 2 represents R-5-8 or 8-5-R, the three represents major or minor triads (depending on the chord type), and so on. (You can add device nuance by choosing ascending triads for a 'red' card and descending triads for a 'black' card.)

- Then work through you chord progression bar by bar, draw a card for each bar and create your 'poor' bass line by writing in the device that the random playing card is assigned to.

Not only will the bass lines you generate be poor bass lines that you can analyze and edit, but the creation process will give you practice in converting devices into notation, which is subliminal practice that will help your sight reading.

There's also a Mental Representations For Bass bonus section that comes with this Volume, and at time of writing I plan to create a number of one page etudes that you can download and correct. Over time these etudes will include 8th note and 16th note lines too, so this will grow into a unique and valuable resource. See Page 95 for details of how to sign up for the online section.

Section 5 - Create Your Own Practice Exercises

As explored in my book *Deliberate Practice For Bass 2.0,* making constant and continuous improvement on the bass guitar (and in any discipline) relies on practice exercises that take you out of your Comfort Zone and into your Learning Zone.

Sometimes changing tempo is all that's required to move from Comfort Zone to Learning Zone. But making exercises more demanding is another way of ensuring your practice is focused on the point where you're learning. A detailed improvement program requires both kinds of exercises.

The second kind of exercise often need to be created from scratch to suit your particular requirements, but they don't need to be created during the practice time that you've got allocated to working with bass in hand. Creating these exercises is a perfect opportunity for 'dead time' practice.

Another form of practice exercise that can be created away from your practice space, and this ties into Section 3 on analyzing bass lines and improving your mental representations of bass lines, are exercises that are designed to assimilate new devices or modifying devices (or other bass line ideas) that have been uncovered by analysis of existing bass lines.

To demonstrate this, here's a practical example working through this process. To start with, here's a two bar, I7 to IV7, bass line that combines using the 8-b7-6-5 device with a modifying device on the downbeat:

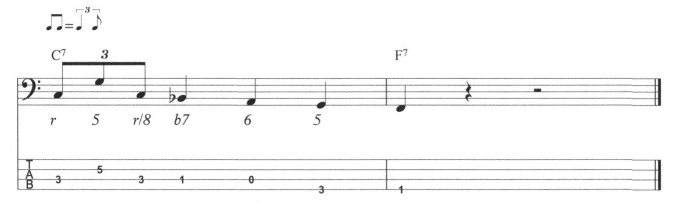

This idea is taken from Groove 14 of my book *Pino Palladino Style Grooves For Bass*. The idea that's been identified for practicing is the use of the R-5-R modifying triplet replacing the octave on the downbeat.

Assuming that this idea has been identified as a piece of vocabulary that I want to add to my toolbox of bass line ideas, then I need to create a series of practice exercises to work on assimilating this.

That two bar fragment makes a good place to start by simply repeating the two bars:

Sidebar: *depending on your precise practice requirements the space on beats 2, 3 and 4 of the even numbered bars could be used to practice another device. E.g. R-3-4-Ch.*

The above exercise could be transposed to other keys, or could be used to accustom the fingers to the plucking hand/fretting hand demands of using this modifying device. Most intermediate level players should be able to play the above exercise a few times and then start practicing this modifying device in other chordal situations.

Here's a 12 bar C7 blues that's built on using this modifying device on the downbeat of as many bars as possible along with the 8-b7-6-5 device, or the 8-b7-6-ch variation:

Because this is a practice exercise there are some interval jumps here that I probably wouldn't use when playing in a real world setting. For example going from low G at the end of bar 4 to the F at the 3rd fret of the D string on the downbeat of bar 5. But the demands of the practice exercise, which is to begin the process of assimilation for this modifying device used with the 8-b7-6-5 device, take priority over real world bass line construction principles.

From here you could either transpose this 12 bar blues to other keys or create an 'origin exercise' to practice this modifying device/device combination.

A simple way to create an origin exercise would be to take the first two bars of the above 12 bar blues and transpose them to all 12 keys:

That practice exercise will quickly allow you to assimilate the R-5-R triplet modifying device in conjunction with the 8-b7-6-5 device. My advice with something like this is to come up with exercises to expand your use of the modifying device (or whatever it is you're working on). In Section 11 on Domain Knowledge I mention that one of the things I learned from a Bass DVD was Billy Sheehan's concept of 'Taking It The Nth Degree' from one of his DVDs.

What that means in practice is when you identify something you like the sound of and want to assimilate into your vocabulary, experiment with different uses and expand upon the original idea.

So to do that we need to identify how the modifying device works. Here's how I would define that:

- The modifying device replaces a root note on a downbeat of a descending device.

- By using a triplet rhythmic variation is created.

- Harmonic variation is created by going from the root to the 5th and back to the root in the space of that triplet.

What I'd now is set up a number of exercises similar to the exercise on Page 46 that let me explore if I like the combination of the R-5-R modifying device with different devices.

For example, here's the R-5-R triplet combined with the 8-6-5-3 device:

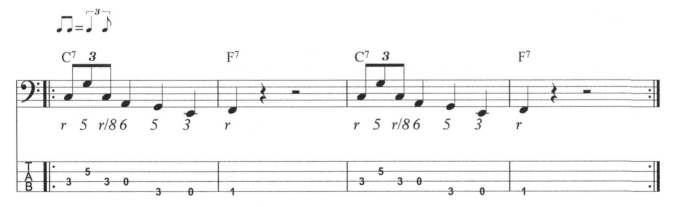

Or here's the R-5-R triplet combined with the 8-b7-5-ch device:

Or you could try the R-5-R combined with the 8-3-4-Ch device to connect C7 to G7:

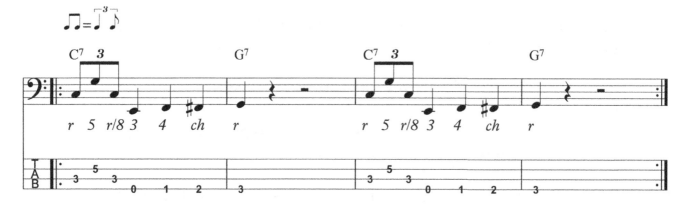

While that works for C because the 3rd is an open string, you'll need it to try it in a key where the 3rd is not an open string to fully test it. In D for example:

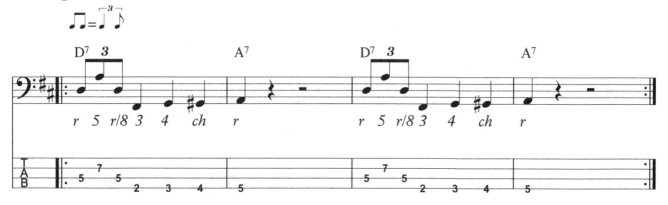

You might decide that's not smoothly playable and only choose to use this combination if the lower 3rd is an open string. But you'll only find that out by creating an exercise to test it, and running that exercise.

Taking It To Nth Degree means experimenting using the modifying triplet with devices going upwards rather than downwards. For example using the R-3-4-Ch version of Device 7 and going up from C to G7:

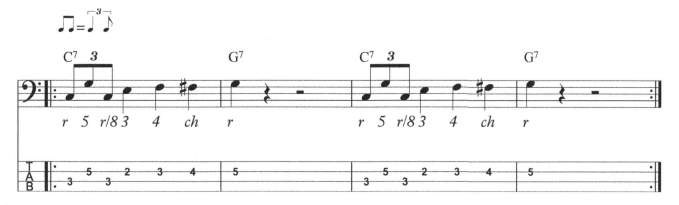

Or you could try combining the R-5-3 modifying triplet with the R-2-b3-3 device which is used to connect C7 and F7:

And you could experiment with other ascending devices, e.g. R-3-5-6, R-2-3-5 and so on. All of these two chord experiments incorporating the triplet modifying device can be created in dead time, and then you can allocate 10 or 15 minutes playing them and deciding what combinations of this modifying device and devices feels good to play and sounds good.

Once you've identified that then you can create longer and more detailed exercises using either common chord progressions or a cycle track (see the examples on Pages 47 and 48) to fully assimilate the combinations that you've chosen.

Advanced Ideas - Taking It To The Nth Degree

There's not space to go into this fully in this volume but here are some other ideas you could try out:

- Inverting the triplet. So instead of R-5-R it become 8-5-8 and combining that with different devices.

- Using the R-5-R triplet idea on different beats of the bar with different device notes. For example play 8-b7-6-5 and play the triplet idea of first device note to the 5th above to different device notes.

- Repeat the previous idea but apply the R-5-R shape to multiple notes in devices...especially linear devices. This can work well to create intense rhythmic and harmonic propulsion at a critical section of a line.

- You could experiment with different notes on the middle triplet instead of the 5th. The obvious one to start with would be the octave. So the modifying triplet becomes R-8-R. If you find a combination you like the sound of....that combination can through a similar experiment as per the R-5-R triplet.

- Try changing the modifying idea from a triplet to another feel. The most obvious idea to me would be to apply R-5-R to a rhythmic combination of two 16th notes and an 8th note.

The goal here is that once you find an idea you like the sound of, you want to experiment with it, and practice with it, in such a way that the idea becomes part of your vocabulary and can be used in multiple playing situations.

Obviously the playing parts have to be done in your practice space with bass in hand. But the creation of the practice experiments, and then turning the successful practice exercises into fuller exercises for assimilation can all be done in your dead time. As a side benefit, creating these exercises will boost your mental representations of bass lines as well.

Section 6 - Rhythm Exercises

In Sections 1 and 2 we worked on exercises to help improve your perception of time. In musician's parlance that's working on your internal clock.

In this section exercises to work on your perception of sub-divisions are introduced. Just like the internal clock exercises, you can do this practice with you bass in hand as well as during your dead time.

These rhythm exercises can also be 'compounded' and instead of using a conventional metronome to give you a basic pulse, you can use some of the metronomes from Section 1 and 2. So you are working both on your internal clock *and* your perception of sub-divisions!

There are three levels of sub-division that I recommend you work on mastering:

- Quarter note and 8th notes with the 8th notes interpreted as even.

- Quarter notes and 8th notes with the 8th notes interpreted as swing feel. Plus quarter note and 8th note triplets if required.

- 16th notes / 16th notes with ties / 16th notes with rests.

To start practicing exercises I recommend a 'metronome track' that consists of:

- A bass drum on beat 1.

- Side sticks (rimshots) on beats 2, 3 and 4.

- Hi-hats that match the pulse you are working on. (So even 8th notes, swing 8th notes or 16th notes.)

There are MP3 tracks for these three time feels in the Bonus Area of the website version of the book at multiple tempos and multiple lengths.

Let's dive into some more detail for each of the rhythmic sub-divisions.

Section 6.1 - Quarter Notes and Even 8th Notes

There are 10 basic quarter note/8th note rhythms that make up 80% of the bass player's rhythmic library with this feel. Those 10 rhythms are contained within this notation graphic:

In the Bonus Area of the website version of the book are five different PDFs that have 50 pages of these rhythms played randomly with 32 bars to a page.

Here's a 24 bar example of these 10 rhythms played randomly:

These are the basic 8th note rhythms. If you count through all the random rhythms in the pages in the bonus PDFs you'll start to get a good understanding of these 8th note rhythms.

There are variations of these rhythms that include rests, and other combinations of 8th notes and quarter notes. In the Bonus Area of the website version of the book are four different PDFs that have 50 pages of these quarter note and 8th note rhythms with rests chosen randomly with 32 bars to a page.

Here's a 24 bar example of what you'll encounter in these five volumes of rhythms:

Section 6.2 - Quarter Notes and Swing 8th Notes

A simple way to generate exercises to practice counting quarter notes with swing 8th notes is to simply print out random pages of quarter note/8th note rhythms, or quarter/8th note rhythms with rests and superimpose a metric modulation sign that instructs the student to interpret the 8th notes as swing 8th notes at the top of each page.

That instantly gives you access to up to 500 pages of rhythms that can be interpreted in this way which are available to download from the Bonus Online version of the book . So you can see how that looks here's the 24 bar example from the previous page of random 8th note and quarter note rhythms with a swing 8th note metric modulation:

And here's a reprint of the 24 bar quarter note/8th note with rests example, but with the metric modulation added:

You could also just write 'swing 8th notes' over the top.

Section 6.3 - Swing 8th Notes With Triplets

Here are all the possible configurations of swing 8th notes with triplets:

These are the basic combinations of swing 8th note rhythms with triplets. In the Bonus Version of the book are four different PDFs that have 50 pages of these swing 8th note and triplet rhythms chosen randomly with 32 bars to a page.

Here's a 24 bar example of these different rhythms arranged randomly for rhythm practice:

One of my often repeated caveats is to ensure that you don't practice exercises because you see them in a book or on YouTube, or heard about them from other musicians. And that instead, you practice exercises that align with your musical goals.

The reason this caveat is repeated here is that the next set of rhythm exercises are probably more suited for drummers than bass players. However as there only three published pages in existence that I've ever seen including triplet rhythms with rests on the triplet notes I thought that for completeness these would be great additions both to this Volume, and to the collection of bonus PDFs in the Bonus Area of the website version of the book.

Here's a 24 bar example that includes quarter notes, pairs of swing 8th notes, triplets, quarter note rests, swing 8th note rests and rests on different sub-beats of triplets. This is a tough exercise to tap out/count through and if you want to truly master the swing 8th note/triplet subdivision you may have to work up to this:

The elements that make this tough are the triplets with rests on different triplet subdivisions.

My advice would be to work on exercises that focus on specific groupings of triplets with rests first first. Here's a 24 bar example that focuses just on swing 8th notes and a triplet where the first note of the triplet is played as a rest. There is a 20 Page PDF in the Bonus Area of this kind of exercise that you can use to count through to assimilated the sound and feel of this specific triplet/rest configuration:

The next exercise is a 12 bar example that focuses on pairs of swing 8th notes and a triplet where the middle note of the triplet is played as a rest. This is the easiest of these triplet with rest configurations to pick up because essentially it's identical to a pair of swing 8th notes but with the first swing 8th note played short rather than long - again there is a 20 Page PDF in the bonus area that focuses on these rhythms for you practice:

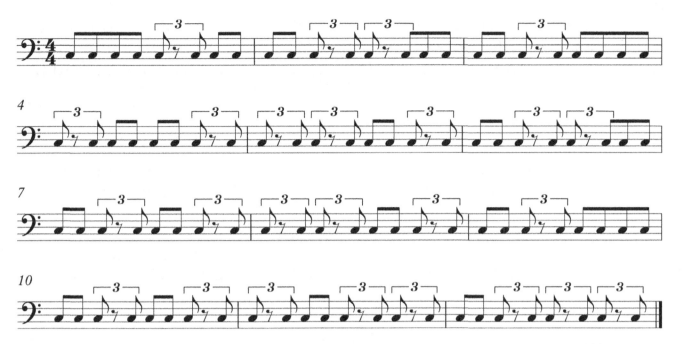

The next 12 bar example focuses on pairs of swing 8th notes and triplets where the last note of the triplet is played as a rest. Again there is a 20 Page PDF in the bonus area that focuses on these rhythms for you to practice:

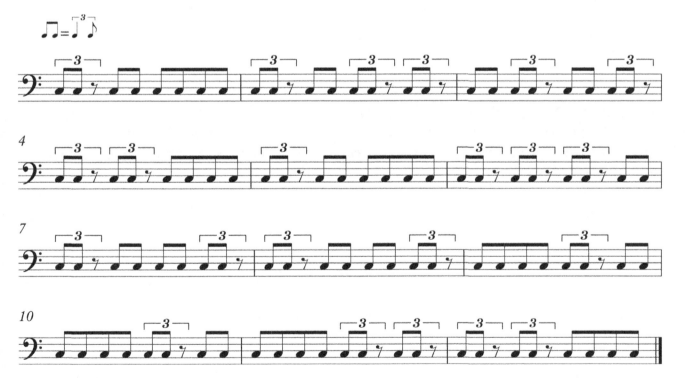

The next 12 bar example focuses on pairs of swing 8th notes and triplets where only the middle note of the triplet is played. So the first and third notes of the triplet are played as rests. Again there is a 20 Page PDF in the bonus area that focuses on these rhythms for you to practice:

Section 6.4 - 16th Notes

There are six basic 16th note rhythms. I cover all the possible combinations of these in my book *16th Note Rhythms For Bass Guitar Volume 1*. Here's an 18 bar exercise that combines these 16th note rhythms in random combinations:

There are four volumes of 80 Page PDFs with random 16th note combinations available to download in the Bonus Area so you've got plenty of music sheets to tap out and count these kind of rhythms.

Section 5.5 - 16th Notes with Ties

Once you are comfortable with the six basic 16th note rhythms, the next task is to practice adding ties to those 16th note rhythmic combinations. Here's a typical 24 bar exercise that contains random combinations of the six foundational 16th note rhythms with ties added in.

There are four volumes of 80 Page PDFs with random 16th note with tie combinations available to download in the Bonus Area so you've got plenty of music sheets to tap out and count these kind of rhythms.

Section 6.5 - 16th Notes With Rests

To master 16th note rhythms you also need to assimilate rests within 16th note groupings. This task is made challenging as shown in the following example that contains two bars of 16th Note Rhythm 2 with rests.

This rhythm is a 16th note followed by a 16th note rest followed by an 8th note. The first bar has exactly this notated out while the second bar shows how this would more likely be notated using a staccato dot:

The second bar is easier to read because groups of 8th notes like this should be a familiar part of your rhythmic vocabulary. And incorporating the 16th note rest by playing the first 8th note in each beat staccato (as indicated by the staccato dot) is easier to comprehend and execute.

In the Bonus Area of the website version of the book there are three lessons, that were part of a comprehensive series on reading 16th note rhythms, that walk through all the permutations of 16th notes with rests incorporating the staccato dot instruction where appropriate.

The short cut version of those three columns is this music graphic that contains 14 different one beat, 16th note rhythmic patterns. The first four bars have one 16th note rest per bar, the next six bars have the possible combinations of two 16th note rests, and the final four bars have the different ways to incorporate three 16th note rests into a beat:

Here's an 18 bar exercises that combines these 14 rhythms randomly with the six foundational 16th note rhythms:

There are four volumes of 50 Page PDFs with random combinations of the foundational 16th note rhythms plus these rhythms incorporating rests (and staccato dotted 8th notes) available to download in the Bonus Area so you've got plenty of music sheets to use to tap out and count these of rhythms.

One note with these rhythms: when counting and tapping these rhythms out, the staccato 8th notes will be counted and tapped identically as if they were normal 8th notes. But if you're *playing* these rhythms, the staccato 8th notes are counted the same but those notes have a 16th note duration due to the staccato dot marking.

Section 6.6 - Advanced Exercises

Bass players occupy a unique position in the band and in an ideal world possess the rhythmic perception of a drummer as well as the harmonic understanding of a keyboard player.

Counting and tapping out complex combinations of rhythms is a great way to work on the rhythmic perception. There are multiple ways to take the kind of exercises featured into this section and extend them to create more sophisticated practice exercises.

Here are some ideas for you - remember that, just like your bass practice, your dead time practice should align with your practice goals:

(i) *Combine Counting Rhythms With The Internal Clock Exercises From Section 1.*

When you're working on internalizing the kinds of rhythms set out in this section, it helps to use a metronomic drum track where the underlying pulse (either straight 8th, swing 8th, swing 8th with triplets or 16th notes) is played on the hi-hat.

Once you've internalized these rhythms with those metronomic tracks, a test of how well that internalization process has been (as well as strengthening your rhythmic perception) is to go back to the start of whatever rhythmic pulse you're working on and tap out rhythms with a track that only provides a click on beats 2 and 4. You're now responsible for counting and tracking all the sub-divisions.

When you can do that, switch to a '2' only or '4' only track.

And then every other bar.

These combinations will hone your rhythmic perception in a way that nothing else does. Plus you've got MP3 tracks you can download with the appropriate clicks and you've got all the Random Rhythm PDF volumes to choose from to work with.

(ii) *Turn The 16th Note Exercises Into Swing 16th Note Exercise By Adding Metric Modulation Markings.*

Depending on what genres you play in you may need to read/play swing 16th note rhythms.

The volumes of random 16th note rhythms can be reused for swing 16th notes simply by printing out pages and hand writing in the appropriate metric modulation sign at the top. Like this:

This also applies to 16th notes with ties and 16th notes with rests. One of the keys of assimilating rhythms is practicing counting out hundreds (and thousands) of bars of random rhythms. All of the 16th note rhythms can be reused for swing 16th notes by adding the metric modulation and interpreting them differently.

(iii) *Using Sub-Divisions To Assimilate Odd Time Signatures*

All of the work on rhythmic sub-divisions has been focused on the 4:4 time signature. There are other time signatures that crop up in rock and pop and jazz. Depending on what genres you play in (or aspire to play in) you may need to be comfortable not only with counting and playing in those odd time signatures, but playing sub-divisions in these odd time signatures.

If by chance you have a copy of Louis Bellson's book 'Odd Time Reading Text' you'll find rhythmic examples like 16th note triplets in 5:4 time or syncopated examples in 3:4 time that include both 16th notes and 8th note triplets.

Most of you reading this volume probably won't encounter odd time signatures and rhythms like this so don't need to practice them. (Remember: only practice what will move you closer to your defined bass goals.)

But bars of 3:4 and 2:4 are common in rock and pop and jazz. And 12:8 is common in blues rock and classic rock and pop. So at the least you'll need to know how to count through and play those time signatures. You'll find 7:8 in funk rock and prog rock (e.g Chilli Peppers and Rush/ Yes). And maybe 9:8 and 5:4 too.

To set up rhythmic exercises to count through in these time signatures and master them, start with quarter notes and 8th notes and then expand from there in a sequential manner. Exactly as has been done in this section:

- Quarter notes/8th notes.

- Quarter notes/8th notes with rests.

- Swing 8th notes.

- Swing 8th notes with rests.

- Swing 8th notes with triplets.

- 16th notes.

- 16th notes with ties.

- 16th notes with rests.

Note that there are rhythmic subdivisions that have been missed from this section for space reasons. E.g. quarter note triplets, 16th note triplets and so on. If you need to assimilate any of those rhythm you can create your own practice exercises (see Section 5) using the methodology used here.

(iv) Play The Rhythms

Tapping and counting the rhythms discussed in this section will help hone your rhythmic precision and awareness of precisely where every rhythmic sub-division is.

Once your rhythmic precision is developing you can also play these rhythmic exercises too. There is a way of doing this in your 'dead time' practice - which, by definition, is practice when you don't have a bass handy.

But there's a caveat.

The way I used to do this was to use a tool that I purchased in the mid 2000s with the absurd name of 'Twanger Prax Ax.' This device was about 6 x 8 inches and had a 'bridge,' four strings of the appropriate thickness, and the strings were about four inches long. What I found I could do with this device was to lay it flat on a table top, make sure my arm was perpendicular to the table top, and physically pluck the strings.

This device was discontinued several years ago but they pop up from time to time on eBay and similar sellers. My advice if you want something like this is to commission a carpenter to make it for you. You'd actually only need one or two strings and a thumb rest!

Sidebar: *my plucking hand technique is predicated on making a straight line from my elbow to my hand so that there's no 'kink' at the wrist, which stresses the tendons (and can lead to RSI or worse), so using this device works for me. Depending on your plucking hand technique this may not be the case for you.*

Section 7 - Schedule Creation And Practice Reviews

In the companion book *Deliberate Practice For Bass Guitar 2.0*, the following activities are detailed as foundational components of a 12 Week Practice Cycle for bass:

- Creating daily practice sheets.

- Creating weekly and monthly practice guides.

- Periodic reviews.

These activities underpin a successful practice plan, but it's crucial to note that they shouldn't take away from time with your bass guitar in hand. Although these activities aren't strictly 'dead time' practice activities, you can treat them as such in order to preserve practice time with your bass in hand.

These are dealt with more fully in the Deliberate Practice book, but they will be outlined here:

(i) Creating Daily Practice Sheets

The main benefit of creating your daily practice sheet before you even pick up your bass is that you start with a clear guide of what you need to practice. If your practice is set up so that the first three to five exercises are relatively easy and relatively quick, then you build momentum into your practice which helps you go through the scheduled exercises and complete them.

Another benefit or creating your daily practice sheet the day before is that no brain energy is expended in having to remember or look up what tempo ranges each of the exercises you are going to do are to be played at. So all your energy can be hoarded and used to focus on your upcoming practice exercises.

From personal experience, I find that creating this the day before works best for me. And preferably after I've finished the previous day's practice.

(ii) Creating Weekly And Monthly Practice Guides

The weekly practice planning sheet sketches out the exercises and activities to be accomplished in the coming week in broad outlines. The detail is filled in with the daily sheets.

The monthly practice planning sheet sketches what exercises and activities are to be accomplished in the coming month. But this is a broad overview, and week to week the specific details may change depending on the actual progress made during the week.

(iii) Periodic Reviews

As well as planning what you're going to practice, you need to review your practice periodically to check what's working, what needs more work, what exercises can be either replaced or made harder because they've been assimilated, and how your practice periods are working in relationship to both weekly and monthly periods and your goals for the bass guitar.

Periodic reviews are also times to adjust your overall plan. Adjustments may be needed because a series of practice activities that you anticipated taking several practice weeks are assimilated more quickly. The converse is true as well, and a series of practice activities may be taking longer than you anticipated they would.

These periodic reviews and adjustments, combined with daily, weekly and monthly practice sheets, help keep your practice dynamic so that it expands or contracts depending on real world progress. The cliche that no plan survives first contact with the enemy is just as true for planning long term bass improvement as it is for conducting military campaigns.

As well as these three activities, one other activity that you can do that sets up your practice sessions for success is to prepare any supporting materials that you will need for those sessions.

This could be printing out exercises that you've created and putting them on your music stand, programming chord progressions in Band In A Box (or your software program of choice), finding practice tracks for specific practice exercises, preparing 'real world' practice tracks using software that creates a mix without bass (e.g. Moises or Song Surgeon), and so on.

Your goal should be to minimize friction in your practice space so that you spend the bulk of the time you have scheduled in your practice space for practicing with the bass in hand actually playing and practicing.

Sidebar: *An eye opening exercise any bass student can do is the following:*

- *Create 60 minutes of practice time.*

- *Equip yourself with a notebook, a pen and* **two** *timers.*

- *Write down every specific bass activity you undertake and the time you spent doing it down to the last second.*

- *When your 60 minutes of 'practice' is up, total up how much time of that 60 minutes was spent on activities that lead to your bass goals.*

- *Activities like tuning up and warming up (and cooling down) don't contribute to your bass goals* **unless** *you purposefully design those activities to do double duty. E.g. instead of mindlessly running up and down scales to warm up, do some fretboard mastery exercises. When tuning up, tune up by ear using a drone for ear training practice. And so on.*

Regular review sessions are an important component of the journey to long term improvement. But treat the time you have available with bass in hand as sacrosanct and do these review sessions when you can't be practicing with your bass.

Section 8 - Device Ear Training

I hesitated about including this section because it's easy to use ear training as a substitute for practice with the bass in hand unless you have clarity about exactly what you're trying to achieve with your bass guitar playing.

My personal preference and recommendation is that most of the ear training you undertake is 'subliminal' ear training. This kind of ear training happens as a natural by product of your practice process.

This is why keyboard players are usually the musician in every band who has the best ears without specifically practicing this. Built into most keyboard or piano practice is a combination of chords, harmony and melody. And that practice serves to help train that musician's ear.

This is one of the reasons why I recommend Band In A Box as a practice tool for bass players. Every practice exercise can be set up so that it has a rhythmic element (either a real world style drum beat, a metronomic quarter note or similar click, or a metronomic drum beat with the hi-hat playing the underlying pulse) and a harmonic element (real world instruments playing chords or just a piano playing a block chord every bar or chord change). There's no reason why nearly every exercise you do can't contain rhythmic and harmonic elements.

But you can set up specific ear training exercises to help improve as a bass player. And doubly so if you spend more than 30 minutes on your own in a vehicle several times a week.

You'll note from the Section Title that I've called this section "Device Ear Training." That's because while traditional ear training has its benefits, e.g. interval recognition, singing scales and arpeggios and the like, the most important musical element for (most) bass players to concentrate on is their understanding of the vocabulary of the bass guitar in relation to playing bass lines to songs.

That vocabulary can be broken down into the constituent pieces found in bass lines in every genre from rock to county to pop to soul and everything in between.

If you've followed me for any length of time you'll know I call this vocabulary '80-20 Bass' and the individual pieces of that vocabulary are called devices.

The kind of practice that I advocate doing with devices, which is codified as 'Origin Exercises,' is not only designed to practice the devices in all keys, but it's designed to be done in such a way that subliminal ear training is a natural byproduct of that practice.

However, if you do spend useful chunks of time alone in a vehicle as mentioned on the previous page then you can set up practice tracks as MP3 files that you can play in your vehicle to supplement the origin exercises that you do as part of your bass practice.

My recommendation would be to set up an 'ear training' schedule that starts out with MP3 tracks containing just two or three basic devices playing in quarter notes against common chord progressions like the 12 bar blues (and variations), the I-vim-IV-V progression, the I-bVII-IV-I progression and so on.

Then as you become familiar with those basic devices you can gradually layer in more devices over time.

If needed, or as additional ear training practice, you can set up MP3 tracks that focus on one specific device and are designed for you to sing the device.

Again you can use a learning progression with these tracks. Start out with tracks where you sing the device being worked on in different keys where you're singing along with a bass sound playing the device. Then create a track where the root note of the device is sounded and you have to sing the device without any support from the track and then in the next bar the device sounds so you can mentally 'check' what you just sang.

To make that clearer, here's a music example of the first graphic imagining that you are singing the R-3-5-3 version of the major triad using the chromatic cycle (and imagine there is a metronomic quarter note pulse playing throughout this track):

Here's how the exercise works:

- The root note (and a chord if you want to add a layer of subliminal ear training) sounds on beat 1 of bar 1. That gives you the key.

- In bar 2 you sing the R-3-5-3 major triad device which is also voiced with a bass sound.

- On the downbeat of bar 3 you can sing the root note of the Db chord - or you can let it sound to give you the sound of the 'key.'

- In bar 4 you sing the R-3-5-3 major triad device starting from Db which, as before, is voiced with a bass sound.

- On the downbeat of bar 5 you can sing the root note of the D chord - or you can lit it sound as before.

- This repeats until you've been through all 12 keys. Depending on your vocal range you will probably need to drop an octave at some part of the cycle exercise.

Here's a music example of how the exercise would work when you feel comfortable singing the major triad without the supporting bass sound and instead using the voiced on the bass major triad as a feedback mechanism so you can compare the sound of what you sang with what it should sound like:

I've marked up the exercise to make it clear what you should be doing and where. But note:

- There are two possible types of practice tracks you can create to to give you 'ear training with devices' practice.

- One type of track is designed for you to listen and identify the device being sounded in each bar.

- The second type of practice track is designed for you to sing the device. If you can accurately sing a device from a given pitch or root note, then you will be able to accurately identify when it's sounded.

In Section 11 I mention a column that Jerry Jemmott wrote for Bass Player Magazine on Jerry's unique ear training methodology called 'Say It Sing It Play It.' I've written a couple of reports on this methodology and you'll find these in the online Bonus version of the book. These reports will give you a way of connecting ear training/singing exercises directly to your bass fretboard.

Sidebar: *The bass guitar has its own vocabulary for playing bass lines. I call that vocabulary 80-20 Bass or The 80-20 Bass Device Method. None of the ear training programs or ear training books that you can find on Amazon or other places teach this vocabulary which is why you have to create your own practice tracks for ear training. There are multiple ways of doing this depending on what software you are comfortable using. It's no secret that I'm a user of PG Music's Band In A Box software and I've found it relatively easy to set up ways of creating these tracks in Band In A Box. That's beyond the scope of this volume though.*

Most conventional ear training methods teach hearing the musical interval between a pair of notes. That does improve your musical hearing but it has little correlation with what bass players are called upon to play for 95% of their playing within in a band context. So it makes more sense to create ear training drills that are aligned with what we're called upon to play. Which creates more familiarity with the bass player's main vocabulary.

As mentioned on Page 78, you can test device hearing against commonly used chord progressions. Not only does this test your hearing of devices, but you also get the subliminal training of hearing those devices used in their correct harmonic context and your musical ear will develop familiarity with the sound of common chord progressions. This will make transcribing much easier because more of the musical elements that go into the transcription process will be familiar to you.

The caveat repeated throughout the book is to make sure any dead time practice you do aligns with your practice goals in the same way that your bass practice should be designed to move you towards the achievement of those goals.

Section 9 - Visualization

Visualization is a technique taught in various sports disciplines that has its place in our toolbox of dead time practice tools.

A well known study often cited when talking about visualization was conducted in 2014. A group of basketball players were tested to see how many free throws they could make.

They were then split into three groups:

- The first group was given 20 minutes a day to shoot free throws.

- The second group visualized themselves making free throws for the same period.

- The third group did nothing.

After thirty days each group was tested again as to how many free throws they could make:

- The first group improved by 24%.

- The second group improved by 23%.

- There was no improvement in the third group, the expected result.

If you want to research the neuroscience as to how visualization works, this link that will give most of the details you need:

https://toat.com/blogs/wellness/visualization-what-science-says

A key point to bear in mind for visualization is that the more you can engage the senses while doing visualization, the more successful that dead time work will be.

How To Use Visualization

I'm going to set up a practical example so that you can actually try this out today to see how it works for you.

The preamble to this is that the main way that I've used visualization is to help learn bass lines to songs. When I was a professional player I often gigged five or six times a week in various settings and needed to know literally hundreds of songs.

Some gigs would require learning the basslines to two or three new songs in a short period of time. Depending on my time constraints, the method I often used was this:

- Take the bass line to the song and strip it to its core elements. E.g. verse, chorus, bridge and so on.

- I would spend some time playing these sections to tempo with bass in hand.

- Then most of the consolidation of the learning, which is the memorization of the bass lines was done with visualization.

- I would burn a CD of the song and have it in my car's CD player. Every time I drove anywhere I would play the songs to be learned and visualize myself was playing the songs.

- I also put the songs onto my various portable devices over the years. Which for most of the time when I was gigging meant a cassette Walkman. Now, you can either add MP3s to your smart phone or, if you're a dinosaur like me, you can add them to your iPod or MP3 player. The process is the same though: when walking or running the songs would be playing and I'd visualize myself playing the songs.

- One byproduct of this was that subliminally I was also learning the format of the songs as well as other song elements like the melody and lyrics.

To you can try this for yourself, I've created a simple 8 bar bassline. It's a quarter note line and uses basic devices. Here's the 8 bar bass line:

For those of you who are familiar with my 80-20 Bass Methodology, here's the example analyzed:

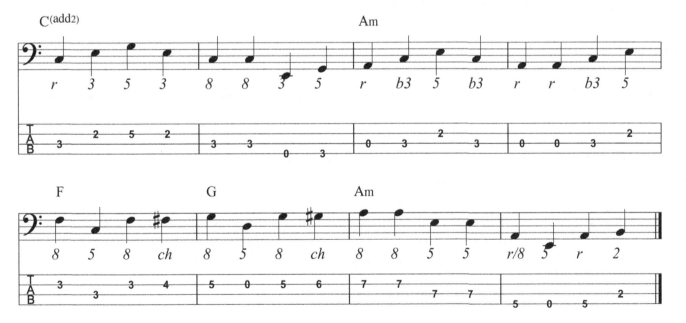

There are two ways to memorize this 8 bar section:

- The first way involves memorizing the notes as you work through the 8 bars. It also helps if you memorize the sound of the bass line as you're working through it originally was well.

- The second way is how I would do this now. (I only started codifying devices in 2012...which was close to when I 'retired' from active playing). Instead of memorizing the notes, I would memorize the devices with the chords. And I'd actually create an 80-20 Chart for myself that looked like this:

If you know your devices this is a superior way to memorize a line that doesn't have to be 100% identical to the original. Not only can you play the appropriate devices on the chords, but you can also make improvised changes to the line easily if you know your vocabulary of devices, modifying devices and connecting devices thoroughly.

Engaging The Senses

On Page 80 it was pointed out that successful visualizations engage the senses.

Here are three potential ways to do that, depending on your exact dead time practice circumstances:

- Listen to the song with the bass line. That way you can hear the bass line as you're visualizing it which reinforces your mental representation of how the bass line sounds.

- Sing the bass line with the track. If you're in a vehicle alone while playing songs you want to learn, this is feasible. Sometimes it won't be.

- Move your fingers as you imagine playing the line. That can be playing air bass, to move the fretting hand fingers. Or, if you have something like the Prax-Ax mentioned in Section 6, or you make one yourself, if you're sitting alone you can listen to your chosen song(s) on headphones and physically play the part with the plucking hand.

So your visualization task is as follows:

- Download the one page 'cheat sheet' plus the practice track with bass and the practice track without bass from the Bonus Section of the website.

- Choose which method of visualization you're going to use: either work on the line note by note; or work on the line device by device.

- Play the line on your bass until you can play it to tempo. Then stop.

- Now move to visualization. Start off by visualizing the sequence of notes or sequence of devices slowly and out of tempo.

- Then use the practice track with bass and go through the 8 bar song fragment multiple times imagining that you are playing the line each time.

- Track how many times you do this.

- After you've clocked up 20 to 30 repetitions then go to your music space, cue up the practice track *without* bass, hit play and play along.

If your visualization was successful, you will find that playing through with the practice track straightforward. Like all practice activities, the more you do it the better you'll get at it.

At one point in the mid 90s I had a working repertoire of around 250 to 300 songs. And visualization was a key factor in both creating this repertoire in the first place as well as maintaining it.

Further Uses For Visualization

The example of visualization given works perfectly for players looking to maintain their vocabulary of song or solidify it. Visualization can be used for other tasks, although always remember the caveat that all practice needs to be aligned with your practice goals.

Depending on your unique goals you may need to devise ways of using visualization that aren't covered here, but I'll suggest three further ways of using visualization:

- *Transcribing Without Your Bass.* In Section 8, Ear Training aimed at learning the sound of devices was introduced. If you're hearing is good enough, you can transcribe from audio straight to notation paper without your bass. And obviously you can then check the accuracy of your 'bass less' transcription once your bass is in hand.

- *Device Practice Exercises.* Just as with fragments of bass lines, you can also use visualization to solidify device practice exercises that you are working on. The only difference is that you're mentally running over exercises aimed at assimilating the playing of specific devices and not bass lines to songs.

- *Fretboard Mastery.* Being fluent on the fretboard is a basic skill that surprisingly few bass players have properly mastered. You can take the three different kinds of exercises I cover in my volume **'Fretboard Mastery For Bass'** and use visualization to help with that practice.

This is only scratching the surface of what you can do with visualization. Don't overlook this valuable tool from the dead time practice toolbox.

Section 10 - Reading Music

Being able to read music is (IMO) a necessity for any bass student who wants to improve on a long term basis.

A substantial part of what goes into being comfortable with reading music and being able to use it as a bass player can be covered with dead time practice. Some examples:

- *Rhythmic recognition*. This was covered thoroughly in Section 6. The emphasis in Section 6 was on developing your perception and accuracy with rhythmic sub-divisions. A byproduct of that work is developing fluency with how rhythms are notated out and how that translates to the bass.

- *Pitch recognition*. Recognizing pitches and rhythms are the two main elements of reading music. You can create pitch recognition exercises where your task is simply to slowly work through each note in the exercises, identify what the note is and visualize where you could play that on the bass guitar. One of the time savers when producing pitch recognition sheets is that adding a different key signature on each clef line changes the interpretation of the exercise. That ties in with....

- *The nomenclature of written music*. The system of music notation that is used today was created hundreds of years ago and has been refined and developed even since. Though the actual pitches and rhythms make up the main part of being able to read music, you also have to understand the nuances introduced by elements like key signatures, tempo markings, accidentals, grace notes, technique markings and instructions to play louder or softer or rise to a crescendo and so on.

Rhythmic recognition was covered in Section 6. If you've worked through that Section and done the kind of exercises suggested then not only will you be equipped with the kind of rhythmic perception you need to function as a bass player, but you should also be comfortable with seeing those rhythms notated out and be able to translate them to the bass.

Pitch recognition exercises can be created in key centres. For example here's a pitch recognition exercise in the key of C (no sharps or flats in the key signature):

Here's exactly the same sequence of pitches, but this time the key signature indicates it's the key of D (two sharps) and every F and every C is sharpened by the two sharps in the key signature:

The same sequence of pitches could be used to practice your fluency with accidentals. Here's the second example with two sharps in the key signature, this time 'natural' accidentals override the instruction in the key signature to play either F or C sharp:

Note that if you played this exercise, and the first exercise at the top of this page, they should sound identical.

The kind of dead time practice you can do to learn the nomenclature of written music is to take music books from your library and work through them, taking note of elements like:

- Key signatures (and key changes).

- Time signatures.

- Start and end repeat bars (including first and second endings).

- Grace notes.

- The use of Coda signs along with instructions to jump back and forwards within a piece of music.

- Markings that signal a change of tempo or a change of feel (e.g. gradually speeding up or slowing down, moving to half time, moving to a swing interpretation of 8th notes rather than straight and so on).

- Notes to be interpreted staccato or to be accented.

- Markings that signal a change of dynamic. E.g. getting softer. Or getting louder. Or played to a crescendo.

The bulk of the work in learning to understand this can be done by working through published music, especially classical music, and where you're not sure about a marking or instruction you can search online to find out the precise meaning and add that to your mental representation of interpreting written music.

If need be you can also create your own exercises (see Section 5) to deepen your understanding of specific markings/instructions and how they are used.

Section 11 - Domain Knowledge

In the original version of *'Practice In Your Dead Time,'* the PDF of which you'll find in the online Bonus version of the book, the concept of your 'domain knowledge' is introduced. The one sentence description of domain knowledge is this:

"Domain knowledge refers to the deep understanding of a specific field or subject matter that allows individuals to perform at a high level and become experts in that domain."

Your practice can help deepen your domain knowledge. And so can your dead time practice.

Here are four dead time activities you can do to help build your domain knowledge:

#1. Read Interviews.

Although Bass Player Magazine is no longer active, you can find back issues on eBay (or you may have a number of back issues in your library) and some of the interviews and features are well worth reading. Here are three examples of things I learned from the pages of Bass Player Magazine that have informed my approach to aspects of the bass:

- Jerry Jemmott - Say It Sing It Play It. Jerry's unique approach to ear training helps you connect the sound of notes in your head with the sound of notes on your bass.

- Lee Sklar - Lee detailed how his approach to the bass came about. Basically he sped vinyl records to 45 RPM so that the sound of the bass was easier to hear and learned the lines in the 45 RPM key. When he played the records at the original 33 BPM he found lots of space appeared in the lines and he improvised ideas to fill up that space.

- Anthony Jackson and others on James Jamerson. There's an issue where Anthony Jackson and other bass players listened to some Motown master tracks of Jamerson's performances isolated and talk about what they were hearing (with musical examples).

Over the period 1991 to approx 2008 there are literally hundreds of interviews and features that are worth reading.

#2. Listen To Interviews With Bass Players

You can find interviews with bass players on podcasts and on sites like YouTube. Most podcasts can be downloaded for listening to in the car or on a walk or on a train. And you can find free YouTube to MP3 converters that will allow you to create your own MP3 files from YouTube videos, and add those MP3 files to your smartphone or MP3 player.

In this category I'd also add Audio Books (e.g. Victor Wooten's two books) and documentaries (e.g. Standing In The Shadows Of Motown). There are some interesting documentaries around on the streaming platforms too, e.g. Get Back by The Beatles on Disney Plus and Netflix has a ton of music themed documentaries (e.g. Clapton, Cream, Creedence, and so on).

#3. Tutorial DVDs

In the 80s and 90s tutorial DVDs were much more of common thing than they are now. Though now there are streaming sites like TrueFire that feature courses relevant to the bass. While most tutorial DVDs aren't great ways to learn in a co-ordinated fashion, they often contain snippets of great interest that can add to your practice approach. Plus listening to the featured bass players can deepen your domain knowledge.

Three highlights for me from different bass DVDs:

- Listening to Tommy Shanon talk about his approach to blues rock on his *'Double Trouble Bass'* DVD.

- Billy Sheehan's concept of 'Taking It The Nth Degree' from his DVD *'In My Humble Opinion.'*

- Rocco Prestia talking about his unique fretting hand system in his 'Fingerstyle Funk' DVD.

#4. Interviews And Tutorial Material For Other Instruments

Although the bass has its own unique musical vocabulary that no other instrument duplicates, there is a bunch of the kind of material already alluded to available for other instruments. Plus interviews with great musicians who aren't bass players. I often use the (true) story of how I came up with the concept of Deliberate Composition by adapting saxophonist Stan Getz's idea (from an interview) that jazz soloing is just composition sped up and played in real time.

Although listening to, and reading bass guitar specific material, will have more of an impact on your domain knowledge of the bass guitar, it's worth remembering that the bass guitar is part of a much larger domain that could simply be called 'music.' If you find you've exhausted your supply of bass related material for building your domain knowledge, then try and find interviews with masters of other instruments on how they approach music and especially on how they practice.

If you've got any close musician friends who are drummers, give them a call and see what tutorial material they've got and check out how drummers approach music. Or depending on your goals, buy some drum tutorial material and see how you can adapt drum exercises to bass.

Section 12 - Playlists

Whatever device you use for listening to music away from your practice space, there are two types of playlists you can create that will add to your dead time practice activities:

#1. Song Playlists.

I use song playlists for going over details of songs to play at upcoming gigs or visualization (see Section 9) or both.

The other important task that listening to the originals of songs you play regularly does is to keep you connected to the original and how it sounds. That is important if the band(s) you play in want the song to sound authentic. It's less important if your band(s) are being looser with their interpretation of specific songs.

#2. Inspiration Playlists.

Committing to improvement is a long term plan. And it's human nature that from time to time the kind of rigorous deliberate practice that's required to fuel that desired long term improvement is hard. One of the peculiarities of deliberate practice - and one of the reasons it can be hard - is that often practice is not a lot of fun.

Sometimes that gets to the point where you don't want to practice at all.

One way to combat that is to play gigs and play with other musicians. The feedback of an audience is one way you can use to keep you motivated to keep your practice schedule ticking over.

Another way is to use an inspiration playlist.

This is simply a playlist on your preferred device that features a number of songs of bass players and bands that inspire you. And preferably, not just inspire you, but are directly referenced in your practice plan.

Then if you get a day where you don't feel like practicing, often due to low energy which undermines low motivation (so eating well, sleeping well, and all those good, but boring, things are a crucial part of your mental and physical state) you can choose not to practice.

But the deal I make with myself, that I recommend that you adopt too, is that if I'm going to skip practice I have to go for a walk and listen to one of my inspiration playlists.

I have three of these playlists. The most commonly used playlist is a collection of Jamerson performances on various Motown songs. The second playlist is a collection of Rocco Prestia lines that I particularly like (though I have a funk shuffle version and a 16th note version). The third playlist is most of the live Rush album 'All The World's A Stage.'

You should curate your own playlist(s) of songs that inspire you. It's a great way to build your motivation to get you back into your practice space with a desire to put in some hard practice to move you another incremental step on your journey to be a better player.

Four Reasons To Sign Up For The Bonus Website Version

There's a bonus online version of the book that you can get by sending a copy of your Amazon invoice to me at this email address:

- paul@how-to-play-bass.com

Please note: *if you bought the book second hand on Amazon market-place, eBay or another second hand online book seller, you don't qualify for the bonuses.*

There are four reasons why you should sign up for this bonus version:

#1. It's free

That goes with the caveat above that you bought the book new from Amazon as mentioned above. It will take less than a minute of your time to email me a copy of that invoice or receipt. Within 12 to 24 hours (usually sooner) I'll add you to the 80bass.com website where the online version of the book is hosted, and send you an email confirming your username and password.

#2. Rhythm Practice.

There are over 1000 pages of Rhythm Exercises in PDF format for you to download and use with the different rhythm practice suggested in Section 6. The only book I've ever seen that has these kind of rhythmic studies is Louis Bellson's book *"Modern Reading Text in 4/4."* The problem with Bellson's book is that it's only 90 pages long and most rhythmic sub-groupings have just a few pages devoted to them. So once you've practiced counting through those pages several times the value of that as a practice activity is diminished because familiarity and repetition comes into play. These downloadable PDFs are worth the price of the book on their own in my opinion...a resource like this is not available anywhere else that I'm aware of. (And if any student ever exhausts this library and needs more...I can create more quickly - all it takes is an email.)

#3. Practice Tracks.

There are practice tracks to download. The most useful ones are the MP3 files that go with the Internal Clock exercises
(Sections 1 and 2). But there are 'rhythmic pulse' tracks as well that you can use to count through the rhythm sheets you can download for Section 6.

#4. Two Libraries Of Sight Reading Etudes.

There are two libraries of Sight Reading Etudes that can be found in the members area. These libraries are constantly being updated. So when you joined - depending on when that is - there may be relatively few entries in each library. Over time though, these libraries will expand.

The first kind of Sight Reading Etude is what you'd expect and you can use these for either traditional sight reading practice OR you can use these for 80-20 Device analysis (as detailed in Sections 3 and 4).

The second kind of Sight Reading Library consists of 'wonky' sight reading etudes. These are etudes that don't quite work. You can print these out, analyze what's going on and what's not working and then rewrite the lines to 'fix' them and improve them. There's no resource like this anywhere that I've ever seen. As it grows over time it will be an invaluable aid to help you improve your mental representations of good bass lines.

So send a copy of your Amazon invoice to:

- paul@how-to-play-bass.com

And I'll get your account set up.

Final Thoughts

For updates, tutorials and 80-20 bass themed material you can check out my main website:

www.how-to-play-bass.com

While I strive to produce an accurate a book as possible I am the archetypal example of a one man band and sometimes typos do slip through. If you see one, please drop me an email and let me know so I can fix it!

Reviews are integral to how books are promoted by Amazon, so if you've enjoyed this book please head over to Amazon and leave a review.

If you've any direct feedback to share with me, please do so.

Stay safe, practice hard, practice smart and strive to be the kind of bass player that other musicians want to play with.

Paul Wolfe
SW England

Other Bass Guitar Books From Paul Wolfe
Available at your local Amazon Store!

Deliberate Practice For Bass Guitar - not all practice is created equally and sadly most bass students don't know the difference between the three different types of practice and equally sadly invest most of their practice time on the two types of practice that don't lead to constant and consistent improvement. This book will go a long way towards helping you identify how you should be practicing which in turn leads to what you should be practicing.

Learning From Paul McCartney Vol 1 - the first in a 2 volume series looking at the playing of Beatles' great Paul McCartney, and the first book to analyze his playing to identify the foundational devices and ideas that he used to put bass lines together in the Beatles early period (up until 1965). This volume covers McCartney's uptempo pop, his 'walking pop,' his straight 8th note rock and roll playing and draws advanced ideas from his 'Rubber Soul' period.

How To Play Bass Guitar In 50 Songs Module 1 - this is the first in a 5 volume series that will give beginners everything they need to practice to go from getting started on the bass to getting started putting their own lines together. The unique '80-20 Bass Device Method' is the spine for this 5 volume series... over the course of the volumes beginners will focus their practice on learning the actual vocabulary of the language of bass and apply that to real world style chord progressions using real world rhythms.

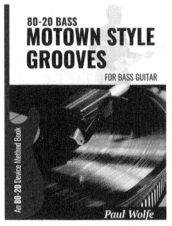

80-20 Bass - Motown Style Grooves - this book isn't a normal 'groove' style book. I define grooves as "fragments of genius" and this book/online package not only contains more than 30 fragments of Jamerson genius, it also teaches and demonstrates all the other information you can get from these fragments. Such as rhythms, devices to approach chord changes, bass line modelling, changing keys, adapting grooves for different genres and more. An essential companion for the Learning From Jamerson series.

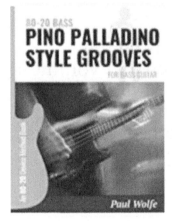

80-20 Bass - Pino Palladino Style Grooves - this book is the second 'fragments of genius' book. This volume takes fragments of genius inspired by Pino's work with John Mayer and as with the Motown Style Grooves book it breaks out the information you can get from these fragments and apply to your own practice to improve your vocabulary, technique and bass playing.

Creating Walking Bass Lines - the best book for bass players to learn to walk is Ed Friedland's first book. Creating Walking Bass Lines is designed as an unofficial sequel to that book and if you've mastered the material in Ed's book, you can build upon that by adding different kinds of walking bass devices to your vocabulary.

Learning From James Jamerson Volume 1 - the first in a 4 volume series looking at the playing of James Jamerson, and the first book to analyze his playing to identify the foundational devices and ideas that he used to put bass lines together in Motown's Studio A. Volumes 1 and 2 start out with the ideas Jamerson used in his straight 8th note lines in the mid 60s.

Learning From James Jamerson Volume 2 - the second in a 4 volume series, this volume builds on the foundational devices and ideas identified in Volume 1. More advanced ideas like anticipations, slash chords, overlapping,indirect resolutions , devices from the 5th and Jamerson's favourite device are all covered. This volume also uses straight 8th note rhythms.

Learning From James Jamerson Volume 3 - the third in a 4 volume series, this volume builds on the previous two volumes and tracks the different methods Jamerson used to layer 16th note ideas onto what were still essentially 8th note lines before his conception of how to play finally took off. (The latter is covered in Volume 4).

Learning From James Jamerson Volume 4 - the final volume in the series, this volume builds on the previous three volumes and breaks down many of the elements Jamerson used in his virtuosic bass lines like Bernadette, For Once In My Life, Darling Dear and literally hundreds and hundreds of other signature performances.

16th Note Rhythms For Bass Guitar - reading and playing 16th note rhythms can seem complex. But there are only six main 16th note rhythmic units. If you practice those units so that you are comfortable with those, and then practice mixing 16th note rhythms together, add in ties and rests, and do it in a systematic manner then it's relatively easy to master 16th note rhythms. The good news: once you've mastered them, you'll never have to work on them again!

Time And Groove For Bass Guitar - because the bass player's role in the band is to connect the harmony instruments with the rhythm instruments (the drums), it's fundamental that bass players have as keen a sense of time as drummers. Most bass exercises though lean on a pulse provided by an external source, either a drummer (whether or in person or loops) or some kind of metronomic pulse (a metronome, sequenced drums). In this book we'll explore how to improve your internal clock by using a drop series and harmonic metronome series with real world style bass lines.

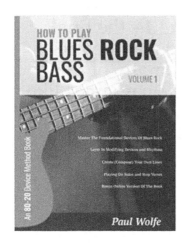

How To Play Blues Rock Bass Volume 1 - the first in a three volume series looking at the devices, rhythms and modifying devices used to play blues rock. Think Pride And Joy, Sweet Home Chicago, Statesboro Blues and a bunch more...as well as the foundational devices this volume covers topics like stop verses, triplet rhythms, playing under solo sections, deliberate composition (create your own lines!), 2 bar devices, Bar 9 devices and more.

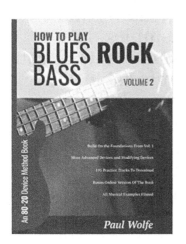

How To Play Blues Rock Bass Volume 2 - the second in a three volume series, this volume builds on the foundational devices and ideas identified in Volume 1. More advanced ideas featured include the Duck Dunn last note triplet, hybrid devices, the rock and roll connection, playing in straight 8th note feel, muted notes and Bar 12 devices.

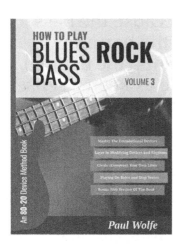

How To Play Blues Rock Volume 3 - the final blues rock volume builds on the previous two volumes and is split into two sections. In the first section, the 12:8 ballad is examined in detail in terms of devices, rhythms and the concept of front end/back end. In the second section advanced ideas for all blues rock lines are featured.

Made in United States
North Haven, CT
18 May 2023